BORN IN THE CHURCH BUT NOT BORN AGAIN

BORN IN THE CHURCH BUT NOT BORN AGAIN

Escaping the Religious Matrix

Lesley A. Francisco

Born in the Church but Not Born Again: Escaping the Religious Matrix
by Lesley A. Francisco

Cover Design by Atinad Designs.

© Copyright 2014

SAINT PAUL PRESS, DALLAS, TEXAS

First Printing, 2014

The name SAINT PAUL PRESS and its logo are registered as a trademark in the U.S. patent office.

ISBN-10: 0-9912242-6-4
ISBN-13: 978-0-9912242-6-5

Printed in the U.S.A.

Contents

Acknowledgements

Jesus Christ: I'm so glad to have finally met You after all these years. You're the best thing that has ever happened to me.

Mom and Dad: Thank you so much for investing in me more times than I can count. I'm humbled that you would see so much greatness in me and take the time to nurture and pull it out of me. I love you ~~all~~ both so much.

Nicole and Lauren: Thank you for always keeping it real with me and helping me pull myself together when I am on the verge of being torn apart. I respect both of you and am appreciative for the inseparable bond that we have.

Grams: Thank you for always confirming that whatever I set my hand to will prosper more than I can even imagine. You and Papa started a legacy that will forever live on!

Caleb McClendon: You personified grace before I even knew what it really was. Dating you has shown me how Christ really loves. Thank you for never having a hidden agenda and loving all of me; I appreciate you.

C3: The best church on the peninsula! Thank you for always having my back, letting me preach to you quite often and actually listening (smiles). I love all of you.

EPIC: Our youth and young adult group. You guys are the reason why I wrote this book. My prayer is that it will help you transition from adolescence to adulthood. I want you to learn quickly what it took me years to overcome, so we can continue to advance the true kingdom of God. The message of grace (Jesus) must be shown to the entire world!

PREFACE

As a young leader, a few of the things I ask God for are wisdom, knowledge and understanding. If I could just have those three things I'd be alright. Well, I think He gave me a dose of those three things so that I could write this book. *Born in the Church but Not Born Again* confronts the lies and manipulation that are often coupled with the gospel of religion. What do you do when you're churched but not changed? There are those of us who are accustomed to routine and not relationship. The religious matrix has held many captive and has depressed, oppressed, and suppressed hundreds of thousands, if not millions of Christians around the world.

My heart aches for those who have been manipulated, heartbroken, mistreated, and abused not only in the world but in the church. We are taught so many rules and regulations and what we have to do to attain and keep God's favor, and that's so far from what

God wants from us. My whole vision and what God placed on my heart for this book is to awaken people from their worldly and/or religious stupor and help them to realize the true and real life that exists in Christ. I personally have a disliking for those who preach more about sin than they do about Jesus. Don't get me wrong and start tweeting about me—I HATE sin, okay? Lesley Andrea Francisco hates sin, but I think we have an issue when we start to teach more on what we can or cannot do, namely, our limitations, as opposed to what God has for us and what we can experience in and through Him. If you really want to know how to quit sinning and get out of a cycle of depression, low self-esteem, and poverty, get more gospel. This good news only comes from and in Christ. I can just imagine how many of us are wondering how do we get out of certain situations or why aren't our lives at the level they should be? Perhaps, we should get to know the Christ of the Bible and not the Christ of the typical four-walled church. I don't know if you've noticed or not, but there's a lot of Christ-less Christianity out here. Even Gandhi said "I like your Christ but I do not like your Christians; they are so unlike your Christ."

I'm a credentialed life coach. I can remember one time coaching with my academic supervisor, Lyn, and she asked how my session with my client went. I said, "Oh, it was great! I took them through this process, but I didn't really understand it because I never did it."

She quickly rebuked me in love and said, "Lesley, we never try to get a client to do something that we haven't done ourselves." It hit me like a ton of bricks, but it was necessary for me to hear that rebuke. That gentle rebuke has stayed with me ever since. Just know that what I am teaching you in this book, I've actually lived myself. It's time out for expecting from others what we don't require of ourselves.

I first discovered this pure message in 2012, and slowly but surely my mind is changing. Think about the difference between something popped in the microwave and something that takes quite a while to bake in the oven. That's where renewing the mind comes into play—things are seeping in and it takes time to learn. I asked God once why we had to renew our minds so much; He replied it was the same thing as having to brush our teeth. Can you imagine going days or even weeks without brushing your teeth? It would be pretty gross. That's the same thing that happens when we don't renew our mind to the truth and freedom that comes from knowing Jesus Christ. The less you feast upon His goodness the more "badness" will occur. Please understand that this whole journey is a process, so don't expect your beliefs to completely shift in an instant. Trust me, those who have overnight success are not usually what they appear. Be comforted in knowing that instant deliverance is not as common as TV makes it appear. There are millions of us who still have to take time to go through the process of life. You are not alone. The true gospel should be so simple that educated, uneducated, old, young, rich, and poor can understand.

Section 1:

FOR THE SAKE OF TRADITION

CHAPTER 1

GROWING UP IN THE CHURCH

The average person growing up in America went to some form of church. I know I did. I'm what you would call a PK (Pastor's Kid). It's almost as if I was born into the ministry. My mom gave birth to me on Saturday, February 3, 1989, skipped church the next day, but was back on the piano the following Sunday with my car seat on the floor next to her piano bench. I'm definitely a church baby. Needless to say, she had to go back to the hospital later on due to some complications most likely due to her not taking ample time to rest. Back when I was growing up, my parents were young in the ministry, so there was no such thing as six-week maternity leave; they had to make things happen. This is a prime example of how doing too much without a break can really take its toll on your body. Growing up in the church, my sisters and I know all too well the "thank you for sharing your parents" praise that comes from other people. I remember how difficult it was for me to even keep friends because it seemed like everyone just wanted to be close to me because of my parents and not because of me. Other guys used to play games in the church to see who could date the "first daughter". Sometimes it was hard finding genuine relationships that didn't backfire. People would often ask my family if we could have meetings, or do conferences or counseling because my parents are pastors.

I know all too well the stress that comes with

being raised in the church and sometimes by the church. When my sisters and I see other PK's, they often reference how their parents or Dad put the church AND the members before them. Although my family was not exempt from the stress of ministry, many seem unable to handle the pressure and simply walk away. I've often heard fellow PK's say things like:

"My dad always makes time for the members. His armor bearer comes to my games more than he does because he's got to go out of town and preach the gospel." "I'm not a people person, but my parents always have people come over the house." Here's one of the things I hear most often from not just pastor's kids, but from church kids in general: "I feel like I have to be perfect all the time; I can just never mess up. It's like I try my best to live a good life, but I can literally FEEL people just waiting for me to fail." These are just some of the things I have heard from other church kids and some of those things I have experienced myself as well. Now, of course, I'm not going to go into detail about which stressors I face the most; just know that the traditional church life is not easy. I'm thankful for parents who can balance the care of home and church life. My heart goes out to all of those who may experience unnecessary stress on a daily basis and who feel like giving up on church and God because of the awful example that has been set at home, or because of the awful example set by a church leader or a church member who has not taken their responsibility seriously and, therefore, has tried to abuse you for whatever reason. You'd think church would be the place where you experience a community of love and peace, but in many instances that is not the case.

There are many people, today, who are bound by tradition. They do things without knowing why they do them. All they know is that's the way it's always been done. Here's an example I've always heard in church. There was a granddaughter who used to cook a ham every year in two separate pots. She would split the ham and put half the ham in one pot and half the ham in the other pot. One day, her husband asked her: "Why do you have to use two pots to cook a ham?" The wife exclaimed, "My momma always did it so that's what I do." The husband couldn't understand why she was doing this so he went and asked his wife's mom. Surprisingly, the mother had the same exact answer as his wife, her mom always cooked it like that. The man was baffled, so he went to visit his wife's grandmother. He asked grandmother, "Why do you use two pots to cook a ham?" Grandmother chuckled and exclaimed, "Baby, I only do that because I never had a pot big enough to fit the ham in!" Finally, the real reason came to light and now everyone knew why every year the ham was cooked in two separate pots. Now that they knew there was a pot large enough to cook the ham in, they never had to use two pots again. When you know better, you do better.

When we stopped having evening services at my parent's church, people thought they had missed God or gone off into sin. My parents didn't know why we were having evening services; but they did know that we were just having them because we'd always had them. That's just what everyone did at the time. They began to pray for insight concerning this issue, and the Lord gave them discernment. When the church incorporated evening services decades ago, people really didn't have much to do other than go to church. They didn't necessarily have both parents working outside of the home like we do now in the millennial generation. Therefore, in previous generations, when they weren't working their land, they were in church. There was always plenty of time to spend with family. Today, we live in a highly sophisticated and fast-paced society in which mothers and fathers rarely get a chance to spend any quality time with their children or with one another. So understand that it's okay not to go to church all the time, but that doesn't mean that you can camp in front of the TV, or work extra or stay on your laptop all evening. Spend those extra couple of hours with your family and get to know them.

My dad told the congregation that he was going to give them his best every Sunday morning so they would never have to get leftovers and go through the motions on Sunday night. Granted, there are some people in certain places who need to be in church every day and night of the week. There are others who have come to a level of maturity in which they are able to receive a Word from the Lord, dwell on it, and keep that Word throughout the entire week. These people don't need to be in church day in and day out. Please do not misunderstand me. There's nothing wrong with tradition in and of itself, but we cannot allow tradition to limit us from receiving what we actually need, which is a Word from God that will strengthen and fortify us. Tradition for the pure sake of tradition leads to ritualism in which people begin to do things just because they are supposed to, and because they don't want anyone talking about them. Don't allow bondage to religion to hinder you from fulfilling all that God has called you to do or become.

CHAPTER 2

(RAIN)CHECK PLEASE!

Is the church still relevant?

We should be careful the way we define relativism. Most people would think having culturally relevant programs and activities will keep people from leaving the church, but I think that's a miscalculation. Many of our Western churches seem to have everything: outreach, state-of-the-art facilities, and a broad range of programs to match any and every lifestyle. In addition to this, there are influential speakers, high quality music, and small groups. If one is truly active in a church like this, how can one become bored? More programs are not the answer, but substance is. So many churches are lacking substance today and wonder why they remain void of true change.

Why are people leaving the church?

Typically, a rain check is something you give or say when you nicely decline an offer, insinuating that you may accept the offer at a later time. In most cases, when I've seen the term 'rain check,' they are left unfulfilled. The Religious Matrix has influenced Christianity to morph into "Churchianity," which is a faith or gospel that is EASY to believe in but extremely difficult to live up to.[1] I went to a Christian college quite a ways from home for my undergraduate degree.

There was a stipulation where we had to attend mandatory chapel twice a week. They also wanted us to attend church on Sunday! I honestly thought that was a bit much. I thought to myself, I don't even go to church that much when I'm at home and my parents are pastors! I didn't go to church while I was in Christian college for the first two semesters—consistently, that is. It was too much. I figured when I got back home I'd get what I needed, and I was right for the most part.

Here are some of the reasons I've received as to why many no longer go to church:

- Boring, routine, and doesn't lend itself to open dialogue.
- It's whack because it starts with dull prayer that someone's heart is not in but they feel obligated to do it. Praise and worship is dull and boring, or it seems like entertainment.
- Church people are judgmental and don't care about your soul, only your money.
- Been hurt by someone in the church.
- Nothing there to keep their attention.
- Witnessed hypocrisy.
- Parents forced religion over relationship.
- No true understanding of God.

There are a plethora of reasons, but I don't even have time or space to get into it all. It just so happens that this group of people is not crying out for better doctrine or clearer theology, but they're looking for love and kindness in a chaotic and haphazard world. People are looking for authenticity. Who can I be real with? Who can I share my story with, or who can relate to me? The truth is, most church people or even Christians in general are separatists. I didn't say ALL, so don't get angry; there are plenty of other chapters in this book for you to get angry about. We have this attitude in the church that says, come in here if you want to be saved and if not stay where you are and go to hell.

We must realize that faith is not to be separated from love. As a church body, we're not to ask them to come in to get the love, but we should go out and love them, and in return they come to us. That's the purpose of reaching. After we reach, we retain. What can we do to keep them? Then we reclaim. We re-present the gospel in its true light and tell them the truth of who they are and who God is.

Another thing that makes church retention so difficult is that we usually leave all the work up to the leader, which leaves no balance. Of course, you have a leader who heads up the vision, but we have to have people who share in that vision and feel they are involved in a communal effort. Many leave the church because they are not required to think. Most churches request that you leave your brain at the door and just accept everything the pastor has to say. There have been many times when church members say, "I would much rather you just tell me what to believe than ask me to think about it. You're the professional—not me. Just tell me and I'll do it." Unfortunately, being told what to believe and how to live is highly desired and sought by many.[2]

Most people who leave the church do so because they hardly ever get to rise above their religious limitations. Many feel they have to suppress their accomplishments, academic study, freedom, or speech for fear that they will not be accepted. Have you ever heard the following: "The Holy Ghost will teach you everything you need to know"? While that may be true, in most cases, religious leaders have used that line to discourage people from thinking on their own or pursuing higher education because they would hate to see someone supersede them. Remember, I'm speaking from a religious standpoint; this is not the case with every leader. In some contexts, you'll find that certain churches admonish you not to read any other texts besides the Bible despite who the author may be. And on top of that, they make sure that you won't deviate from the KJV. I like to tell people whom I come in contact with that God doesn't speak to me in King James English. He speaks to me in a way which I understand very clearly.

Let's not forget, people also leave the church

because of the many scams and scandals that happen all of the time in the name of God. There are people who have left because of significant abuse within the four walls of the church. I met a group of girls once at a fashion show and about three of them told me how they would never step foot in a church again because a deacon or church leader molested them and also tried to do the same to some other family members. The thought of that conversation makes my stomach turn, not just because those religious leaders committed heinous acts, but because those girls now have a terrible picture of who Jesus really is. Sometimes, it's not even what others did to them, but it's the judgment that people face that may cause a temporary or even permanent leave from the church.

Is there hope of return?

Unfortunately, there are believers, today, who do not call upon Jesus because they believe the lie that they have no right to do so. They are so blinded by judgment, condemnation, and feelings of bitterness. There are those who think that their mistakes have disqualified them from calling out to God for help. Some may even believe that they don't deserve God's help and blessings because they have stayed away from church so long and failed to attend regularly, read their Bible, or pray every day.

When we are feeling down, ~~and~~ out and struggle with our feelings of unworthiness, we don't need a preacher to tell us what is right and what is wrong, or give us a list of do's and don'ts; we need a Savior.[3] We must get out of the religious mindset that tells us that we have to clean ourselves up before Christ can use us. We need a Savior who delights in meeting us right where we are no matter our present state or condition. You cannot earn by your own effort His desire to save you. It is by His grace! When this message is really grasped by the institutional church, there won't be enough room to hold all the people who will want to come and hear the gospel.

Section 2:

ESCAPING THE POWERS
OF INFLUENCE

CHAPTER 3

DELIVERANCE FROM THE OPINIONS OF PEOPLE

Many people misunderstand the concept of 'deliverance'. We think the only people who are delivered are those who have been strung out on drugs, those who have been extremely promiscuous, or those who tarry at the altar all night until demons are cast out in the form of foaming at the mouth. No. Deliverance is simply reconciling your soul back to God, where it was originally intended to be. Therefore, being delivered from the opinions of people takes the focus off what they say and think about you and puts your attention back on God, the Creator.

Bound by Society

People can also be a major source of limitations; they can bind us like shackles. How many intelligent young people have purposely become underachievers just to be accepted by their peers? How many adults have lowered their ethical standards just to be accepted by someone they considered impressive? They don't realize that they, too, have been shackled. When your hope and trust is placed in anything outside of God, you've allowed yourself to be shackled; you've limited what God can do in your life. When you trust your job instead of God to meet all of your needs, you've been shackled. God gave you that job as an avenue to acquire finances, but it is He who gives you the power to get wealth. He never meant for your job to replace the trust you have in Him, because if your trust is in that job, you will lose your mind if you lose that job. When your trust is in God, you can be told by your boss that you're going to be laid off, and you'll say, "That's all right because it's in Jesus that I live, and move, and have my being. This job is just an avenue."

We live in a cruel society that operates under the tenet that the only good news is bad news. Many have been ostracized and alienated due to its doom and gloom forecasts. Others have been limited in their endeavors because of negative forces that exist. Proverbs 18:21 says, "Death and life are in the power of the tongue: and they that love it shall eat the fruit thereof." I believe that one of the reasons we have so much poverty, murder, and crime in our society is because reports about these things are perpetuated by a media that constantly speaks death into the lives of people. Our media is continuously broadcasting alarming statistics: the divorce rate is up; the homicide rate is up; the suicide rate is up. They have influenced us into thinking: Everywhere you turn, people are killing one another, so you can't go anywhere after dark! You've got to be fearful! You've got to be cautious! You've got to be suspicious!

A society which thrives on negativity can keep you from becoming all that God has purposed you to become, because one negative word can change your life forever. One word can ruin your life. One wrong statement can change your destiny. One negative thing said by someone in a passing moment can touch you at the very core of who you are like a spear hitting a mark. One such statement made a dramatic impact on my life for some years.

When I was in middle school, someone said I couldn't sing. Guess what? I believed it. For years I claimed I couldn't sing and would often lip sync because I didn't think that my voice was good enough. Actually, I waited until I was a junior in high school to sing again. Another scenario that affected me pretty badly was being told by various men that God didn't call a woman to preach. I used to be so ashamed to tell people that I was going to school to become a preacher and often debated changing my major to interpersonal communications just so I would never have to put myself in uncomfortable situations. Usually what we believe is only someone else's opinion that we've accepted and incorporated into our own belief system.[1] That's why it is so important to become an independent thinker, void of the opinions of others. My mother often says: "Those who do not discern your worth are disqualified from being in a relationship with you." I believe that now.

It took a few years to realize that people are not in bondage because of past traumas but they are in bondage to the lies they believed as a result of past traumas.[2]

Many Christians get mixed up when they start trusting in people and things instead of trusting in God. When we come to the realization that it is in Him that we should trust, then we are released from the limitations of man. Man will say you can't get anywhere; you're nobody, and God can't use you. You must understand, however, that you operate according to a higher authority and by a higher calling placed upon your life. Once you recognize that higher calling, in and through Jesus Christ, you will refuse to be oppressed by people. The Apostle Paul said it like this in Galatians 3:1: "Who bewitched you?" What Paul was asking the Galatians is what I ask you today: Who tricked you? Who fooled you? In the same manner, I ask you this: Who pierced your heart? Who vexed you? Who, with their negative words, shackled you at a young age? Who told you that your daddy was nothing and you weren't going to be anything and that no one could ever love you? Who told you that you were going to be a deadbeat like your dad or that you would be an unfit mother? Who told you that you couldn't become a doctor? Who told you that you would never get into a certain college? Who told you that you would die from cancer? Who told you that you had to live in poverty the rest of your life? Who told you that you have to stay on welfare? Who told you that you always have to receive food stamps, or struggle with pornography, or fail in business? Who tricked you? Who limited you from fulfilling the destiny that God placed in your life? Who told you these lies and why did you believe them? The lies that bewitch and bind many Christians spring from three primary sources of limitations: tradition, people, and society. Elements from any of these areas can bind us, and thus keep us from moving forward in the things of God.

Forgive and Flourish

One of the ways to escape the societal grip on your life is to forgive, which literally means to grant relief from payment. Unforgiveness causes torment. You'll think you're fighting devils and demons because of the call of God that's on your life, but sometimes it's really just pride and refusal to admit that you're bitter towards what others have said. To live with bitterness is to live a life of misery. You must be humble enough to admit that you are hurt and offended. Now, I'm not talking about old time testimony service where you get before the whole congregation and confess. I am talking about confiding in a trusted friend, leader or better yet, Jesus! Confession really is good for the soul but it must be in the right context. Forgiveness is not a feeling and it often takes time. You may very well still remember the event, but the sting of bitterness and rejection will be gone. Sometimes the memories can be aggravating, but it's just like a bumblebee with no stinger—it's all noise. Remember, recovery takes time; it's a process. One way to ensure you have begun your forgiveness process is to pray for the person who has offended you. I have to dispel this myth: Just because you forgive does not mean that you have to allow that person the same amount of access they had before. Yes, reconciliation is great but it is not necessary in all cases. Sometimes you have to tell people that you will love them from a distance. In other instances, reconciliation is very much necessary. It just depends on the situation. There is no cookie cutter answer to hardly any scenario, which is why you need your own relationship with the Lord, and His Spirit will tell you what it is you need to do. It takes a mature person to forgive. Maturity does not come easily; if it did, no one would hold a grudge.

Through forgiveness, it's possible to become emotionally mature. This means that what people say or do cannot really annoy or aggravate you unless you allow it to. Forgiveness is essential to total healing. To refuse to forgive yourself for whatever you may have done is simply spiritual pride. If you're having a hard time forgiving, affirm this right now: "I completely and freely forgive _____; I release them mentally and spiritually. I am free and they are free! I wish nothing but the best for them all the days of their life. I do this with a great attitude, in love and with no remorse. All the blessings of life I pronounce upon them. Today is my day to be free and I receive that freedom now!" Every time that person comes to your mind I want you to lovingly say, "I have released you and the joy of life is yours." It may not be automatic, but those seeds you continually plant will in fact manifest, you just watch. Lovingly release the past. Free your prisoners and you will indeed escape your own mental prison. After doing so, continue to feed your mind with positive, life-giving thoughts. This is a very serious matter. Your subconscious mind cannot take a joke, which means it takes you at your word.[3]

As you continue to feast on life-giving thoughts, your past will dwindle away.

What are some life giving thoughts?

CHAPTER 4

THE PROBLEM OF SIN-CONSCIOUSNESS

Bound by Limitations

I'm sure at one point in time you've asked yourself, "Why is it that when I get right to the brink of success, I feel like I go backwards? How come every time I try to do something good, I don't? Why is it that just when I think I'm right where God wants me to be, an obstacle gets in my way?" These experiences have led many to develop a circus elephant mentality. I know what you're thinking: "What in the world is that?" If you go to a circus, you'll notice that massive chains do not restrain the elephants. A single, small chain attached to their ankle binds these huge wild animals. As you compare the strength of one of these elephants to that of the little chain that binds him, you think to yourself, *If this elephant wanted to, he could break loose and run over people all day long. How does that little chain keep him constrained?* It isn't the chain that holds the elephant but it's the elephant's mind that has him bound.

When circus elephants are born, their legs are bound with a chain that is driven into the ground with a stake. The baby elephant, unable to break that chain, is helpless to free himself. Every time he goes so far out, the chain stops him. When the baby elephant becomes a mature adult, he is capable of easily breaking the chain, but by this time his mind is doing what the chain is now inadequate to do. Conditioned into thinking that he cannot break the chain, the elephant has long ago quit trying. Whenever he feels the chain tugging at his ankle, he simply stops, thinking that there's no need for him to try to go any further. In the same manner, there are many Christians with this mentality today. There are children of God whose minds were bound by the powers of the enemy when they were young Christians, and now that they are mature saints, they don't realize that they possess the power to break free from the limitations that have them bound.

As a young Christian, there were things that had you chained down. Bad habits, negative confessions, and unregenerate thinking most likely had you bound, and every time you tried to move beyond these things, you were pulled back. Now that you've reached a degree of spiritual maturity and you begin to understand Scriptures more, you can now more easily demolish those demonic mindsets that hold you back. Remember in my introduction I told you the three things that I asked God for: wisdom, knowledge, and understanding? Well, the Bible states in Hosea 4:6 that God's people are destroyed for lack of knowledge. Christians are not destroyed so much for a lack of intellectualism, not so much for a lack of academic training, but the problem is that there are a lot of people with a ton of natural sense, but they've missed out on spiritual sense.

This may not sound so nice, but understand that

UN REGENERATE MEANS

one can be intelligent and at the same time stupid. A person can be intellectual, but lack the sense necessary to handle every day affairs. I've met my share of intellectuals who are academically astute but lack common sense. We are failing to achieve those things that our forefathers, who had virtually nothing, were able to achieve. Many of our forefathers were able to take very little and accomplish great tasks for the Lord. They led awesome revivals, made a tremendous impact on their communities, and tore down demonic strongholds. Today, we who have an ocean of spiritual and natural resources and knowledge at our disposal, yet we are not accomplishing these things. Why? Because we are trying to fight spiritual battles with carnal weapons. We are looking at our circumstances and fleeing the battle because of fear. We are believing the lies of the enemy. We are allowing ourselves to be bound by our unrenewed minds.

Condemnation Will Kill You!

Condemnation is what you feel when you try to become righteous through the law, or in essence, try to do everything right in your own strength and fail. It is the negative emotions that are left after you failed to keep the rules perfectly.[1]

When you blow it, the devil will be ready to use God's law as a weapon to condemn you because he knows that if he is able to put you under condemnation, you will feel like a failure. I remember while in my late teens praying for <u>God to cleanse me of the same sins over and over and over again</u>. I would pray myself to sleep. I would kick, scream, cry, and beg for God to show mercy upon me and not send me to hell. Even human impulses such as a <u>sexual thought</u>, or the urge to want to curse someone out, or throwing a banana peel out the window had me feeling guilty and condemned to hell. I had it bad! I remember praying for over ten years straight the same exact prayer every night <u>for hell insurance</u>. I remember having rapture ready races with my younger sister in which we would pray the fastest we could: "Lord, please forgive me of all of my sins in Jesus name, Amen." I definitely remember what it felt like to <u>get saved monthly</u> or to never feel like I was good enough not knowing the truth is, I'm not good enough, <u>but</u> Jesus is perfect enough and His perfection makes up for my flaws any day. Not only did I condemn myself, but also I often would project my imperfections and shortcomings on to others. <u>If anyone else appeared less than holy, I had a problem</u> with that; I was quick to judge.

I struggled with condemnation so badly that I used to get sick all the time. Much of that sickness came from stress and negative thoughts I had about myself. When you are under condemnation, fear, stress and all kinds of sicknesses will follow. When I let

43

condemnation rule my life I was rude, I was bitter, I was angry, and those signs manifested themselves in the form of sickness and disease. I was an unloving and unforgiving person. I thought to myself often, how am I supposed to love people who hurt me? Then when I was mean and hurt others in return I would beat myself up about that too. I was living in hell, since that is in fact what self-condemnation is. I was such an extrovert at the top of my game and all of a sudden I became a shy, boxed in hermit. People would say things like, what happened to you? You've changed! I even remember being so deep into religiosity that my dad made me fast from Christian TV. I got into the mindset that anything that wasn't blatantly Christian was a sin. All I watched was preaching and worship and it really got worse because I became even more confused because not everyone on television preaches the same gospel.

Oh, but when the gospel of grace (unmerited favor) and God's unconditional love became a reality in my life, something changed—not outwardly, but inwardly. I had such an overwhelming peace; I still do to this day. You can hear something over and over again but never really get it; I got it now. I've accepted the truth. I finally understand the saying, "The truth will set you free but first it will make you mad." Before, I was keeping tabs on my sins, now I'm keeping tabs of my righteousness. I'm not conscious of sin anymore;

I'm conscious of the Son, Jesus Christ. This Son-Consciousness has produced a holy zeal for the Lord, godly character, discipline, and more fruit than I could have ever imagined.[2] I'm not saying that I never make mistakes, but when I do I don't go into depression about them anymore.

?as we age in Christ should we be seeking Wisdom

Hyper Grace

Those who feast upon the glorious finished work of Christ are usually called cheap or hyper grace preachers because those who don't understand a full revelation of grace think that it can be abused and people will go off into sin for fun. I'm not so sure that there is such a thing as hyper grace. You can't preach too much grace. Hyper grace doesn't hurt you but hyper holiness can. People go on a tangent believing that because grace is preached people are going to sin and do whatever they want. If you believe that way, I'm not sure you've captured the essence of the message. Then again, I've talked to countless people, who grew up with laws upon laws about how they have to do certain things for God to love them, and let's just say they've got a lot of issues.

Grace is not a doctrine; it's the person of Jesus Christ! Can you preach too much Jesus? So to all those who think grace is such an awful thing to preach, I ask you this: What's the difference between someone who says they can go out and party all night because they're under grace compared to someone who lives morally upright but is still full of pride and arrogance? Don't we all believe that sin is sin and it doesn't matter what form it's in? Sometimes I wonder if people truly believe that. For example (this one may be a tough pill to swallow), What if people held signs on the street corners that said, "God hates fatties" just like they hold signs that read "God hates faggots"? A lot of us would be in trouble. Everyone is in need of the grace of God! The problem I have with the claim that the "message of Grace" leads people into sin is that our definition of sin is often out of whack, and relies more on tradition than it does the person of Jesus. Sin is not about what's in your glass cabinet or Blu-ray collection; it's about love or a lack thereof. Don't spend your life micromanaging the morality of others, or living every moment in a judgmental state.

There is so much more to knowing Christ than going around with your moral magnifying glass, seeking out sin and questionable behaviors. I've got news for us: emptying the buffet trough after Sunday morning service (gluttony) is a thing spoken against in the scriptures more than most of our other pet sins. Yet, somehow, we rarely speak against it, or call it "sin". Can the "message of Grace" lead people into sin? Of course, it's possible; any message can. But is it? I'd say much less so than people assume, since much of what we call sin is not sin at all.[3]

Focus on your position and not your condition

You may be asking, how can I get to the place where I don't struggle with condemnation or sin and I have super-abounding peace? When a believer is struggling with sin, it is a case of mistaken identity. Whatever you think you will become. If you think that you are a person whom God can't forgive or love, you'll feel that way and you'll live a miserable life. If you think that you will continually reap bad things in life, then that is exactly what you will manifest. On the contrary, the more you believe that God loves you and that you are righteous apart from what you do, the more you will live in peace. Always remember that God is not mad at you, but He is mad about you. The quicker you catch a revelation of Jesus and how much He loves you, the better. If you believe right, you'll live right.

WHAT IF A BUTTERFLY LIVED ITS LIFE THINKING IT WAS GOING TO BE A CATERPILLAR FOR THE REST OF ITS LIFE?

Think about that for a second. A butterfly certainly is a caterpillar, but it's not destined to stay that way. In the same manner, what has been spoken to or about you may be true, but it is not the TRUTH.

You are not defined by what you deal with but by the word of God. Forget your addictions; focus on God. If you are a born again believer you are not your sins, but you are the righteousness of God in Christ. You will have what you say! (Proverbs 23:7) If you keep saying, I'm an alcoholic, I'm a drug addict, I'm a homosexual, I'm a porn addict, I'm a glutton, I'm a dead beat, I'm an unfit mother, you will become just that. If you don't want it, don't say it! Now, it's okay to acknowledge that you have hang-ups and that you have struggles, but don't perpetually condemn yourself by mentioning them over and over and over again. If it's not helping you to change your outlook or perspective, then it's hurting you! Always tell yourself that you are the righteousness of God in Christ. I don't care what you're dealing with, what you're struggling with, or what you think you'll never overcome. Continue to tell yourself that you are righteous. Right thinking does in fact equal right believing.

When we give credence to the opinions of other people or the devil, life seems to make circumstances appear larger than they really are. What we focus on or give our attention to the most becomes our reality. **THE DEVIL WANTS YOU SELF-CONSCIOUS, BUT GOD WANTS YOU SON-CONSCIOUS.** The devil can block how effective you are as a Christian if he can convince you to believe that you are a product of your past. James 4:7 promises that the devil will flee from you if you can submit to God. An obsession with right and wrong makes people self-conscious instead of Christ-conscious.[2] If you perpetually live in a state of obsessing over right and wrong, you will live a very frustrated life. A sure way to live a defeated lifestyle is to try to focus on the sins that you don't want to commit. When you finally want to stop living a frustrated life and being in a constant state of fear, you will focus on your righteousness with Christ and that alone. Keeping your attention fixed on Him is what keeps you in perfect peace (Isaiah 26:3). Don't focus on your setbacks, on trying to be godly, on your morality, or on anything else. Just focus on Jesus!

Godly sorrow vs. worldly sorrow

Luke 22:31-34 New Living Translation (NLT): *"Simon, Simon, Satan has asked to have all of you, to sift you like wheat. But I have pleaded in prayer for you, Simon, that your faith should not fail. So when you have repented and turned to me again, strengthen and build up your brothers." Peter said, "Lord, I am ready to go to prison with you, and even to die with you." But Jesus said, "Peter, let me tell you something. The rooster will not crow tomorrow morning until you have denied three times that you even know me."*

Another thing the devil will try to do is make you

feel like you can never overcome your failure. Let me show you how by comparing the disciple Peter with the disciple Judas. There can come a trial or test so big that it is strategically designed to take you out of this life. Sometimes we also fail those tests of life, but Jesus wants us to live through those failures. Just because you made a mistake that does not disqualify God from loving you. Peter made a pretty large mistake. I mean, what's worse than denying Jesus three times when you know that you know Him? See, whenever you encounter a personal failure, this is a prime time to fight the good fight of faith. Faith is knowing that throughout any type of failure that the Lord Jesus is praying for you just as He prayed for the disciple Peter. The temptation that the enemy has at stake for you and your life is not you committing a MORAL failure, but that you deny the very existence of God.

The enemy wants to let the negativity of life be your identity, and you have to literally purpose in your mind that you will not let the event that happened in your life define you because if you are defined by your circumstance the enemy has won. Why do you think it's so important for Jesus to say I'm not praying you don't fail but I don't want your faith to fail? We have to pray about these things so that our faith will grow in the midst of our test. Peter denies the Lord three times. Now think about it: Being associated with Jesus back in that day was almost a crime. It's obvious if you get caught you're going to die too! So Peter's angry and cursing and he just keeps on failing. But look at the comparison between the two disciples. Peter failed, but his faith didn't fail. Judas failed not because he turned Jesus over, but he didn't stop there. He let his sorrow drive him mad; he feels crushed and he kills himself. So Judas' faith fails. It's interesting, Jesus prophesies to both of these men: to Peter, you're going to deny me; to Judas, you're going to betray me. But after Judas' failure, he never repented. Peter had a godly sorrow that led him to repentance without regret (Romans 2:4), but Judas' sorrow led him to suicide.

Section 3:

THE BORN AGAIN EXPERIENCE

CHAPTER 5

WHY YOU NEED A SAVIOR

The danger of mixing covenants

There are two major covenants in the Bible: the Old Covenant and the New Covenant. After understanding this, I trust a message of hope will be received. Before Jesus died on the cross, man was subject to the law. The law was very strict; there were many rules and regulations that had to be followed in order to "obtain" righteousness. The law is perfect, but people are not. Even though it still seems the same today, before Jesus came, man was almost always concerned with, what do I have to do to be right? How do I get it right? What will make me right? I don't ever want to be wrong. Those who were religious and tried to live under that law never truly had a sense of fulfillment, because they were always looking for an answer of some sort to be fulfilled or to attain right standing before God. In the Old Covenant sin was not forgiven or absolved; it was atoned! Back in that time the process of forgiveness had to be repeated over and over and over again. The law was never able to provide perfect cleansing. Because of this, God wanted to get rid of the Old Covenant altogether (Hebrews 8).

When God issued a New Covenant for us, Christ came and cleansed us ONCE and for all time when He died on the cross, thus He will never have to die again. That's how good His death is. God's will was never to have an animal cover our sins. His will is for us to be made holy once and for all by the blood of His Son, Jesus Christ (Hebrews 10:10-19). Now, we live under a better covenant with BETTER promises. Once we got born again and accepted Jesus Christ as our Savior, His commandments are now written on our hearts. No longer do we live under the condemnation of the law, we are now a product of grace. The law is all or nothing. You must keep every jot and tittle. If the law hadn't been given, no one would know what sin was. That's like telling your child, when you get older don't go drink, and don't start smoking! They probably never even thought of doing those things, but because you brought it to their attention now they're curious. It is the same thing with the law of the covenant; it arouses sinful passions. That is what it was designed for—to show how sinful you truly are.

Live the two, fulfill the ten.

Mark 12:30-31 New Living Translation (NLT)
And you must love the Lord your God with all your heart, all your soul, all your mind, and all your strength.' The second is equally important: 'Love your neighbor as yourself.' No other commandment is greater than these."

God's new law is in no way meant to be burdensome. All He asks of us is to love God completely and love our neighbors as ourselves. These commands are not something God just randomly made up. Loving God and people date back to the time of the Old Testament (Deuteronomy 6:5, Leviticus 19:18). When you love God completely and care for others as you care for yourself, then you have fulfilled the intent of the Ten Commandments and the other Old Testament laws. Prior to Jesus giving us the two greatest commandments, He was approached by the religious leaders of the day who, in their own estimation, tried to outsmart Jesus by asking Him several questions about the law to see if He would answer correctly. Jesus was vexed by their love of vain tradition, preeminence, fanfare, and outside appearance. The thing that's most thought provoking is, those who were most knowledgeable about the things of God turned out to be the farthest from the kingdom of God, while those who were blatant sinners and penitent tax collectors who never observed the law were much closer to the kingdom.[1] Remember, it was the religious people who wanted Jesus crucified.

I'm really hoping that this book will challenge the religious mindset and destroy the sacred cows that religion has to offer. Religion is not the most terrible thing on earth, but it is not the most positive either. Religion has some sort of matrix in which it enslaves and binds people to its system. We say many sins can be an abomination to the Lord but so can religion!

(Amos 5:21) Jesus viewed religion negatively as is evident in the New Testament. On more than one occasion, He rebuked the religious leaders of His day. There has never been a time when Jesus spoke more harshly than when He had to rebuke the Pharisees. He called them "blind leading the blind" and "white-washed tombs" among many other terms. Little did the religious leaders of the day realize that Jesus' two commandments summarize all God's law. Let His commandments rule your thoughts, decisions, and actions. When you are uncertain about what to do, ask yourself which course of action best demonstrates love for God and love for others. This is truly the only way to effectively live life.

There's a serious mixture going on in the body of Christ. People want to have a little law and a little grace simultaneously because they feel that they need to have earned God's approval instead of just receiving it by faith. That doesn't work. It's like oil and water, they don't ever mix. Try proportioning or balancing those two and see if it works—it doesn't. Jesus even told us that you don't put new wine (New Covenant) into old wineskins (Old Covenant). If you continue to mix the two, you will end up looking like the majority of the church today: confused, frustrated, Gnostic, and with very little power, if any.[2]

There is no balance

I'm not sure why so many Christians are still trying to balance law and grace. If you are for the law, be all for the law. If you are for grace, then be all for grace. Pick a side! Why do you think Jesus also said: "I know thy works that thou art neither cold nor hot: I would thou wert cold or hot. Because you are lukewarm, and neither cold nor hot, I will spit you out of My mouth" (Revelation 3:15–16)? What Jesus did when He died on the cross at Calvary has become the tree of life for us in the New Covenant. Now we are able to live a victorious life every day without fear, guilt, condemnation, or shame. We no longer have to worry about the tree of good and evil, wondering if we taste the forbidden fruit will we be condemned forever. Jesus has made it so that we can feast upon the tree of life, His finished work. So if you're living under the heavy weight of condemnation and are dealing with judgment or fear, you can toss it and know that it is not the gospel of Jesus Christ.

The significance of the finished work

Today's church is obsessed with Christ's second coming, but has yet to fully grasp the power of His first coming![3]

JESUS WAS FORSAKEN SO YOU DON'T HAVE TO BE FORSAKEN. While Jesus hung there on the cross, He cried out the opening words of Psalm 22: "Eli, Eli, lama sabachthani?" That is, "My God, My God, why have You forsaken Me?" (Matthew 27:46) Understand that the physical sufferings of Christ are not the reason our sins were paid in full, His body however did pay the full price for our healing. Our sins were paid in full because when Christ was on that tree, God the Father crushed His only begotten Son. It is also the moment when the Father's presence left Christ alone at the cross where He bore our sins and became a curse. This is the first time that Our Lord Jesus addressed the deity as God whom He called, Abba or Father, but never God. At this time of forsaking, Jesus no longer felt that Fatherly compassion. At this juncture, God was no longer a father to Jesus, but he HAD become a judge. Most would note the Scripture that says the Father is too holy to look upon sin (Habbakuk 1:13).

Now, we see that Jesus literally BECAME sin, though He was sinless. If I may make that plain for you, I might reiterate that although Jesus was sinless, He became sin. Whether you are dealing with homosexuality, lying, fornication, idolatry, greed, etc., Jesus paid the price so that you would not have to. What Jesus has done for us however does not make it "okay" to partake in these sins because His sacrifice would be in vain if we had a free pass to live however we choose. Jesus' death empowers us to want to live a life free from sin, whatever that may be for us. What about the scriptural teaching that the Father is too holy to look upon sin? Now, let's not get carried away with that. The Father is too Holy to look upon sin and not do something about it. If God would have rescued Jesus, our sins would have never been paid in full. Many of the things we deal with in our personal lives He became, so that through Him, we don't have to sin.

Now, when we face the generational curses and other sins that try to take us out, be assured THEY CAN'T because when Jesus became a curse for us He gave us the ability to use His name to be delivered from those sins and wayward lifestyles. Here are two questions for reflection: (1) Have you taken the time to consider that Jesus was abandoned by the Father so that you might not be abandoned by Him? (2) What do these words from the cross mean to you? For the first time, Jesus literally EXPERIENCED hell. What is hell? Hell is complete separation from God. Because He experienced it, we can escape it! Thank God that Hell does not have to be our future home.

The story doesn't end at God being forsaken; it ends when He said, "It is finished." "When Jesus, therefore, had received the vinegar, he said, It is finished: and he bowed his head, and gave up his spirit" (John 19:30). Jesus is now confirming the promises He had previously stated. The sufferings and agonies in redeeming man are over. The toils and boils in the ministry, the persecutions, mockeries and labor pangs of the garden of Gethsemane and the cross are ended, and man is redeemed with an everlasting righteousness. It Is Finished! *TETELESTAI* is the perfect indicative mood of the Greek verb *teleo*, which means "to bring to an end" or to complete.[4] What does this show us? The perfect tense shows us the action was completed in the past with results continuing in the present; the results are still in effect today! The indicative mood lets us know the act that took place is an objective fact and that the work Jesus finished was definite and real. This lets us know what Jesus spoke was initiated in the present, but it had the power to terminate our past! *Tetelestai*! It is finished! Did you know that this Greek phrase was also written on business documents or receipts in New Testament times to show that a bill had been paid in full? There's nothing that you can do to add to or take away from this glorious truth!

The cross of Christ provided forgiveness from what we have done and deliverance from what we were.[5] By Jesus' one sacrifice, you and I were made perfect forever! In order to obtain grace, a heavy price had to be paid. Jesus literally had to die and shed His blood for us to walk in grace. Once you receive a revelation of the grace of God you will NEVER look at it as a license to sin. When you understand the HEAVY price that Jesus had to pay for you and me, all of a sudden a strong desire to live right will consume your life. The truth will make you free, but first it will make you mad. I was so upset when I found out that I wasted years of my life trying to earn the grace of God. It took a while to write this book because I thought it might be controversial. We can't be scared of a little controversy; the grace of God must be proclaimed vehemently to all the nations of the earth! It is the devil who tries to put the thoughts in our minds that we have to work to be in right standing with God. "The thief comes only to steal and kill and destroy; I have come that they may have life, and have it to the full" (John 10:10).

Interestingly, in that verse, Jesus was actually talking about false teachers. Don't worry. This can allude to Satan and his works as well because Satan never wants sound doctrine in the church. It's crazy that this passage is talking about teachers of the Word of God who come to deceive the flock, manipulate, take revenue, and steer people away from Christ. He was even speaking of the Pharisees and false teachers who came to steal the hearts of people from God and kill and destroy the souls of men by wrong teaching. Jesus doesn't want anyone under a thief's ministry. He comes to give real life without manipulation that will draw you to Him. What is an abundant life? Abundant means, existing or available in large quantities, plentiful.

Whether you're a believer or not, you can live an abundant life. A drug dealer can live an abundant life; he can have all the money, clothes, cars, and property, but this is not life to the full. And it's not life with eternal security. It may be temporal, but it is not fully satisfactory. The only way to effectively live the abundant life is through Jesus Christ. Jesus came that we might experience life to the FULL!

The true Gospel is the finished work of Christ! "He made him who knew no sin to be sin on our behalf, that we might become the righteousness of God in Him" (2 Corinthians 5:21). "But Lesley, I still feel guilty," you may think perhaps. Because of sin, guilt will never be wiped away! You will never be cleared from guilt. Everybody is always trying to get cleared from guilt. Let me explain. In the eyes of Jesus, it's not that you're going to have your guilt removed; it's that you're going to die. (Romans 6:1-11) If you don't die, you're still guilty. The ONLY way you're not guilty is if you are IN Christ. If you're not IN Christ you will ALWAYS be and feel guilty! But as long as you're trying to live right, be right, do right, fast, pray and try to get God to do something, you're still trying to exert and enforce your own righteousness. It's like saying, 'God, I know I'm this filthy person, but I'm going to do right and clean myself up to the point where I believe God is going to accept me and I am worthy to be saved and used.' It's the absolute worst thing you can do in God's kingdom, and

⌐ do what?

65

moreover, it's considered abuse to yourself. The key is to submit to God, give up your will and die with Christ, then you are hid in Him and it's no longer you (Galatians 2:20).

The only way we can be free is if we give up our life for His! When you are dead you are no longer bound to the law, which is rules and regulations saying what you can and cannot do. According to the law, if you do right by it, you'll receive single blessings but if you do not, double cursings (Deuteronomy 28). The law is for those who are living (Check Romans 7). The point of the law is for man to come to the end of himself and see his need for a Savior. The Bible says that we are free from the law. Let's take a husband and a wife for our example. A wife is bound to her husband only when he is living. In sickness, you're bound to that person. In poverty, you're bound to that person. Through diseases and trials, you're bound to that person. Marriage is 'til death do you part. In marriage, partners stick together.

It's the same with the law and humans. You're bound to the law as long as you live! So if broken relationships want to hit you, it can. If debt wants to show up, it can. It's not until you die (and I'm not talking about a physical death) that you are no longer bound to this law that is so attracted to our sinful nature. You must die to your own will and take up the will of Christ. The will cannot be put into effect until the death is confirmed (Hebrews 9:16-18). When a relative or someone dies you cannot access their assets until you give over the death certificate. You have to prove the death in order to receive your wealth.

It is the same way with Christ: He has already died, His blood has been shed, and until you confirm that you have died to the things of the world and to the things of the flesh you CANNOT access all the assets and benefits that are FREELY given to you in Him. His will is located in the Bible. He already wrote everything that He has made available to you and He wants you to have it now, but you've got to do your part and die to your flesh.

What is the flesh? The Bible is not telling you to kill yourself physically, but it does imply quitting self-sufficiency. The biblical term for 'flesh' is meeting your own needs apart from God. "Walking in the flesh" means that you are trying to rely on your own ability instead of Christ's. No one ever said that this would be an easy task. God's purpose in this humbling process is to bring you to the end of your own resources so that you will be ready to understand that He is the only source you need.[6] If we want God to use us in any capacity, we cannot put confidence in our own strength.

It's so important to note the freedom that comes from being dead to sin and alive in Christ. The old has gone and the new has come (2 Corinthians 5:17). You have now become unidentifiable with the things of the world. Because you are hidden in Christ, those lies of the past can't find you anymore. In His eyes you are a new person. It's those crazy friends and relatives you have to worry about now. And when those temptations come back, remember, it's not you! Now, many of us still think, well, I still feel bad, but if you're **IN** Christ, He specifically told me to tell you TODAY that it's okay to walk out in your freedom. A dead person doesn't feel bad for things they've done in their past, because they have no feelings. Those are fleshly thought patterns that must be renewed in the spirit of our minds. The New Covenant is the finished work of Christ. The only work we have to do as Christians is to labor to enter into His rest. (Hebrews 4:10) Why are we commanded to labor to enter into His rest? It's hard to do. It means you cease from your own works. This type of labor requires utter humility because it says I can't or I did absolutely NOTHING to deserve this. And the laboring part isn't just getting there, but it's staying there and continually knowing that it's not by your work or effort.

How I got my "but" back.

A highly debated topic in Christianity is, "Who will make it to Heaven?" I think the best answer would be, it's none of our business. God is God and we are not. Christians must stop putting people in Heaven and hell when they have no authority to do so. I will say, however, that by calling on the name of Jesus, Heaven will be a lot more populated than we think. Here's a scripture that many like to quote:

Don't you realize that those who do wrong will not inherit the Kingdom of God? Don't fool yourselves. Those who indulge in sexual sin, or who worship idols, or commit adultery, or are male prostitutes, or practice homosexuality, or are thieves, or greedy people, or drunkards, or are abusive, or cheat people—none of these will inherit the Kingdom of God. Some of you were once like that. But you were cleansed; you were made holy; you were made right with God by calling on the name of the Lord Jesus Christ and by the Spirit of our God (1 Corinthians 6:9-11).

The most powerful 'but' on earth is the cleansing of that of Jesus Christ. Let me give you the definition:

'But' is derived from the Greek word *Alla*, which means nevertheless, notwithstanding, an objection, an exception, a restriction, nay, rather, yea, moreover, it forms a transition to the cardinal matter.[7]

'But' is a conjunction, a cliffhanger, if you will, something that's used to NEGATE the previous clause. The transforming and cleansing power of Jesus Christ is so real and powerful that He has the complete and absolute power to negate your previous situation or struggle and MAKE you an entirely new creation in Him!

Isn't that good news? See, grace inspires us to share a person and not a plan. That person is none other than Jesus Christ.

What About the Wrath of God?

The wrath of God is very much real; it is not a made up concept, but perhaps, it is a misunderstood one. Christians should talk about the wrath of God, but it should not dominate our conversation. God's wrath is certainly revealed from Heaven against all ungodliness according to scripture (Romans 1:18, 2:5). However, God gave us His Son, Jesus, so that no one would perish. Christ does indeed deliver us from the wrath that is set to come (1 Thessalonians 1:10). Does God's wrath exist? Absolutely, but it is not how you may have been trained to think. Think about the wrath of God as the frustrated anger of a disappointed lover and not that of an unappeased deity or judge.[8] God's anger lasts only for a moment, but His mercy endures forever. Martin Luther explained that wrath is experiencing God's love in a state of disobedience. God's wrath is not to be equated with human wrath. God's wrath is tied up in His love and holiness working in conjunction. If God were not a holy God, humanity's disobedience would not bother Him. In the same manner, if He did not love the way He loves, sin would not serve as offense to Him. Sin is not merely breaking a law, but the rejection of Jesus Himself. Jesus wants His kingdom full of repentant sinners, but those who exclude His invitation will be rejected (Luke 14:23-24). Wrath is not completely negative. In fact, it is rooted in the love of God. Even though God may condemn a person to eternal punishment, it is not because He wanted to; it is the sinner who freely chooses damnation. Therefore, hell is not a prison in which people are longing to escape, but it is a sit-in where sinners have barricaded themselves to keep God out.[9]

The good news is that the bad news you've probably heard all your life about God is not true! I'm here to challenge the way of thinking that claims only a few will be saved. Through the revelation of Jesus and His finished work, I have a very optimistic view of salvation that is rooted in the love of God for all humanity. It's the love of God that can bypass all religions, no matter what you believe, and cause people of other faiths to uphold Christ as the Savior of humanity. Even the Apostle Peter had a change of heart. He exclaimed that he realized that God does not show favoritism but accepts those from every nation who fear Him and do what is right (Acts 10:34-35). Peter was one who was very judgmental in nature and thought that his way was the right way but God has a way of humbling us all. In His love, however He gives us a broader vision and helps us see more clearly.

Many Christians are so negative about how wide

the mercy of Christ is. They debate over issues such as baptism, the Holy Trinity, what you can and cannot wear, but Christ is concerned about your heart. It is the soul that will be saved, not the body. I wish people would understand that God sent Jesus to be the Savior of the world and not just a preselected group. The finished work of Christ is God's grace toward sinners. Christians who are in pursuit of holiness may ask, if salvation is going to be so large, then is grace just a cop out? A resounding no! To pursue holiness is to have the desire to be Christ-like. Jesus saves us by grace to be holy, not because we got our lives together on our own. Jesus does not want you to love Him because you believe He serves as your hellfire insurance. Your mission should not be to witness to other people simply because you believe that He will send them to hell. If that's what you believe, you've missed the Gospel. Jesus is so much bigger than hell. He did not come to condemn the world but to save the world (John 3:17). However, we must realize that anyone can reject that saving power of Christ. I believe that God is actively working to ensure anyone who is truly seeking Him will find Him before death and have the opportunity to be saved.

SO, WHAT DOES IT MEAN TO BE BORN AGAIN?

Born again experience

John 3:3: "I tell you the truth, unless you are born again, you cannot see the Kingdom of God."

In this chapter, I want to help you understand what Jesus describes as the born again experience. Let's look into John 3:1-18 and I'll do my best to explain where I think questions would arise.

John 3, New Living Translation (NLT)

There was a man named Nicodemus, a Jewish religious leader who was a Pharisee. After dark one evening, he came to speak with Jesus. "Rabbi," he said, "we all know that God has sent you to teach us. Your miraculous signs are evidence that God is with you." Jesus replied, "I tell you the truth, unless you are born again, you cannot see the Kingdom of God." "What do you mean?" exclaimed Nicodemus. "How can an old man go back into his mother's womb and be born again?" Jesus replied, "I assure you, no one can enter the Kingdom of God without being born of water and the Spirit. Humans can reproduce only human life, but the Holy Spirit gives birth to spiritual life. So don't be surprised when I say, 'You must be born again.' The wind blows wherever it wants. Just as you can hear the wind but can't tell where it comes from or where it is going, so you can't explain how people are born of the Spirit."

The characters of the Bible are a lot like us. Just like Nicodemus, I'm sure many of you are wondering the same thing. How in the world can I go back into my mother's womb? What does it mean to be born again? When you are tired of religion as usual, it's time for you to have a born again experience. Those who desire to be born again care not about the state of affairs, sacramental rituals, or temporary pleasures, but that of their soul and its salvation. Jesus is signifying here that birth is the beginning of new life. It entails having a new nature and affection. The first time we entered into the world, we were born in sin and shaped in iniquity.

Jesus informed Nicodemus that each human being's real need is to be born a second time. He wasn't trying to get this Jewish leader to turn over a new leaf, try harder, or to polish his lifestyle, but He was addressing the issues of the heart.[1] Many think Christianity is either a behavior improvement or monitoring program, but Jesus shows us that God's plan is to exchange our carnal nature for His godly nature. When we are born the second time, we are made new creatures and we are vastly different from what we were before. What about the water and the spirit part? These are two words that express the same thing. Water is figurative here for the grace of God.[2] The notion of water and the flow of the Spirit was a prediction of Ezekiel before Christ came (Ezekiel 36:25-

27). First, I think it's important to note that it is impossible to even understand what Jesus did for us without the ministry of the Holy Spirit. When we are born again, the Spirit does something for us, which we cannot do for ourselves. Despite Jesus saying, don't be surprised, you can imagine Nicodemus was quite astonished at the things Jesus said about being born again. Above all, the born again experience is very much spiritual in nature. Even Jesus Himself says that it is like the wind; you can't explain it, just know that it takes faith to know that it exists.

"How are these things possible?" Nicodemus asked. Jesus replied, "You are a respected Jewish teacher, and yet you don't understand these things? I assure you, we tell you what we know and have seen, and yet you won't believe our testimony. But if you don't believe me when I tell you about earthly things, how can you possibly believe if I tell you about heavenly things? No one has ever gone to heaven and returned. But the Son of Man has come down from heaven. And as Moses lifted up the bronze snake on a pole in the wilderness, so the Son of Man must be lifted up, so that everyone who believes in him will have eternal life. "For God loved the world so much that he gave his one and only Son, so that everyone who believes in him will not perish but have eternal life. God sent his Son into the world not to judge the world, but to save the world through him. There is no judgment against

anyone who believes in him. But anyone who does not believe in him has already been judged for not believing in God's one and only Son."

There is Biblical proof that God loves you whether you are saved or not. God did not send His Son to condemn the world but to save the world. You see all the judging that God was ever going to do was placed on Jesus when He died on the cross. For this reason, if we believe in Him and we are in Christ, it is impossible for us to be condemned (Romans 8:1). Jesus died for the whole world, but that does not mean that the whole world is automatically saved. Each individual must make a personal decision to receive Jesus as his or her Savior. Being born into a Christian family does not automatically mean you are a born-again believer, anymore than going into a garage makes you a car! Every person has to make a personal decision to receive Christ as his or her Savior. You cannot live off your parents' faith or your pastor's faith; it's a personal choice. People will believe in anything and everything, but can only come to a living faith in Christ Jesus through the gift of the Holy Spirit. If we revisit Jesus' conversation with Nicodemus you'll see Jesus says that Himself. (John 3:5) Remember when we talked about Jesus uttering His final words on the cross, "It is finished"? Well, that's when He gave up His Spirit. Jesus gave up His Spirit so that He can live in you!

The purpose of the Holy Spirit

The Holy Spirit is not a thing, He is a person; He is God. People mistakenly think of the Holy Spirit as a condemner and a spiritual police officer when the Bible actually calls Him a comforter and a counselor. The purpose of the Holy Spirit is to lead believers into all truth. Confusion occurs when believers read the Scriptures out of context and do not research whom the speaker is speaking to. All of God's Word is written for our benefit, but not all of it is written to us. The Holy Spirit will never call you a hypocrite, or unworthy; that's the devil's job. Satan, the accuser, is the one who whispers condemning words and thoughts into your mind making you feel like you're not good enough for God. As a comforter, however, the Spirit is here to comfort you and to point you back to what Jesus accomplished on the cross every time you fail. The only thing that He will convict you of is your righteousness in Jesus Christ! I'm sure you're wondering, if the Holy Spirit doesn't remember a man's sins, then who does? I heard someone once answered, his wife.

It's not that the Holy Spirit is forgetful of your sins, but pure love does not keep record of wrongdoings (1 Corinthians 13:5). Your evil deeds He remembers no more (Hebrews 10:17). The Holy Spirit doesn't convict you of your sins but of your right standing with God. How can someone convict you of something that they do not remember? Be encouraged. He is not waiting for you to slip up and fail time and time again, and if you do fail He's there as a constant reminder of God's love (Romans 5:5). Also, the Holy Spirit is not this thing that is far off in a distant land; He lives inside of you. Take comfort in knowing that He doesn't come and go as He pleases, but that He dwells within you and stays with you (Romans 8:11). I think it's important to know that the Holy Spirit does not play hide and seek just for fun. If you want the Spirit you can have the Spirit. You do not have to fast and pray in order to receive the Holy Spirit. Just ask (Luke 11:13). Believing in Jesus is the only requirement to receiving the Holy Spirit (Acts 2:38).

What about the unpardonable sin?

I'm sure you grew up hearing that if you blaspheme the Holy Spirit you are going straight to hell. I remember asking what that meant and someone told me that it was saying that the Holy Spirit is of the devil. Ever since I was made aware of what blasphemy was, I started getting these thoughts in my head about the unpardonable sin. Those thoughts wouldn't go away and they would replay over and over in my head and I just knew that I was doomed. If, like me, you're worried about committing that sin, you most likely will not. Those who would ever commit such a sin would have no feelings of regret; they wouldn't care. Here's what you need to understand: there is not one sin that a Christian is not forgiven of. When you receive the revelation of why God sent the Holy Spirit, you will understand that the unpardonable sin is simply to consistently reject Jesus! The Holy Spirit came to testify of and witness about Jesus Christ (John 15:26). To blaspheme the Holy Spirit is not a one-time thing, but an ongoing attitude of continually rejecting the person of Christ of whom the Holy Spirit testifies. Also, just because your sins and lawless deeds are not remembered that does not mean that you can go out and do as you please. The Holy Spirit enables you to live a godly life. In fact, it's impossible to live a holy life without the help of the Holy Spirit. He's an illuminator. If you're ever reading the Bible and you don't understand a particular passage, He will help you to understand it. "He will bring all things to your remembrance.".

Birth Trumps Behavior

When you start preaching the good news religious people get mad. It's crazy how many people really would rather profess a bad Gospel. It takes a lot to shake the paradigm of the western mindset. Not only does Jesus love you, but He likes you, too! Birth, not our behavior, determines our identity. There are certain limitations that hold us back from becoming all that Christ has called us to be. Some have been caught up in the religious matrix of oppression and negativity. Deep down on the inside, you know that there are great things within you, yet, there is something that keeps you from going any further. When you get ready to step out, there's always something tugging and holding you back; the matrix has you in its grip! Thank God for Jesus because He can destroy the matrix. He's able to lift off what others have placed on you and what the devil has tried to steal from you. He's able to remove the burdens and destroy the strongholds that have been placed upon you by tradition, people, and society. Jesus came to preach a word that would loose and repair the lives of those who were broken and bound by humanity.

The Bible says He was able to do this because He was anointed by the Spirit of the Lord (Isaiah 61:1). So, if you want to escape the religious matrix, if you want to be set free, you need to get the anointing— Jesus. You need Jesus to help you get out of this matrix. You need a new birth. If you don't have Him or understand what He's done for you, you'll never truly escape the prison that you're in. Religion cannot destroy yokes or burdens; it only creates them. It is the anointing that breaks yokes. Because of Jesus you don't have to be bound by religion, you don't have to be bound by oppression. You don't have to conform to the world. You don't have to accept the negative things that were spoken over you. Your burdens can be lifted. Jesus says take my yoke upon you, for my yoke is EASY, and my burdens are light. Grace is not achieved, but it is received. Your theology does not have to be perfectly worked out in order for God to love you or for you to be accepted by God.[3] The only person you have to convince that God loves is yourself. You don't have to pray for hours a day getting God to pour His Spirit out on you; He's already done that. Believe and then you will receive. It is as simple as that. Most people don't believe they are worthy enough to embrace a God-given identity so they reject what God says about them. It's not humility to disagree with God; it's humility to believe what it is He says about you.

Choosing Change

ROMANS 12:1-2 MSG

So here's what I want you to do, God helping you: Take your everyday, ordinary life—your sleeping, eating, going-to-work, and walking-around life—and place it before God as an offering. Embracing what God does for you is the best thing you can do for him. Don't become so well-adjusted to your culture that you fit into it without even thinking. Instead, fix your attention on God. You'll be changed from the inside out. Readily recognize what he wants from you, and quickly respond to it. Unlike the culture around you, always dragging you down to its level of immaturity, God brings the best out of you, develops well-formed maturity in you.

Life is not just about being born again; it's about renewing your mind. You can be born again and still live a mediocre life. In order to see the fruit of everything Jesus died to give you, you must renew your mind. You are the only person who can renew your mind. No one else can do it for you. Not your pastor, your friends, your parents, or even Jesus; you must put in the effort. Renewing the mind is not easy. It takes rewiring and repentance. Repentance is very much a process of learning and unlearning and relearning and renewing. It's not a word that deals with sin as much as it is something that deals with our mindset. We are transformed by the renewing of our minds. To re-new means to get back to thinking like new, how we were intended to be, like Christ. When you accepted Jesus into your life no one pressed the delete button on your memory. There are still certain strongholds that you may have to overcome. Strongholds are simply fleshly thought patterns that were ingrained into your mind when you lived your life apart from God.[4] To overcome limitations you must have an all out truth encounter with the word of God and apply what you have read daily to your life.

You are what you eat. What you take in spiritually

will eventually start to show outwardly. Every time you read the Bible, it is not going to be Skittles and Hershey bars. It's full of good news, but remember everything that is good for you may not taste all that great—just like vegetables. There are certain vegetables that I can stay away from my whole life even though eating them is really good for me. I'd encourage you to get a Bible. I recommend the New Living Translation version because it is simple and easy to understand. Second, pick a place to read your Bible on a consistent basis. It could be in your room, at your office, on your couch, in the back yard—wherever. I'd then challenge you to pick a place in the Bible to read. Obviously from my notes in the book I would suggest starting with the New Testament, either with the gospels or the epistles. The gospels tell us who Jesus is while the epistles tell us who we are in Christ. Last, don't be afraid to ask questions. I've finally come to the understanding that it is okay not to know the answer to everything.

The me I was meant to be

If there is one thing I could get people to understand it would be that life needs you. Your life matters; you are significant. Did you know that you could live in a state of permanent purpose? One of the greatest offenses to God is not being who He called you to be. One of the things I have come to understand is that every time men and women try to advance, every time we try and move forward, every time we try to do something great for God or even for society, there are things that stand in our way and try to limit us from doing all that God has called us to do. I'm certain our vulnerability to hindrances can be because many Christians don't know their purpose.

There are certain assignments that God has given each of us. Everyone has been called to do something. Whether you ever fulfill that calling or not, it's there. Also, if you're going to do something that God has not called you to do, no matter how much money you are making, no matter how great that something is, no matter how much success you are having, you have missed God's calling or His best for your life. For instance, if you were called to be a doctor and you ended up being a preacher, you blew it. You missed God. If you were called to be a preacher and you ended up being a doctor, then you still missed God. I recognize my calling as a preacher and I know the good Lord blessed me with the gift of gab to proclaim His grace to the nations. People will always try to fine-tune your calling for you.

Here's the scenario I often receive. My parents are pastors and people often ask me: Did they force you to go into ministry? Why are you at their church? Why can't you just go start your own ministry? I have had others to try and get me to branch off and do my own thing separate from them, but I know what God assigned me to do. I know for a fact that I'm not called to be a church planter. Some are just gifted for that. Why would I go and build my own church when I already have a solid foundation laid and I can just grow from where I am? That's silly. I almost fell for that a couple times, but I really had to seek God for myself. I'd be most miserable if I listened to most of the people who told me what I was called to be before I consulted with God.

Now, I'm not saying that people are always wrong, but what they say should very well line up with what God has already been speaking to you about. Don't EVER let someone influence you against your will or the will of God if you have not heard Him clearly. Be patient and listen; He will speak to your heart. When you recognize your calling, you can get into the stream of what you were called to do, and you can fulfill that calling with joy. Knowing your purpose enables you to overcome limitations that will inevitably present themselves to you. It is very important that each Christian finds out what it is that God has called him or her to do.

Closing Words

CAN JESUS HAVE
HIS CHURCH BACK?

Escaping the Religious Matrix

As Christians, we have an obligation, and it is to show others how to become true followers of Jesus Christ whether they become baptized members in our church or not! I'm sure you're wondering, "Does that mean I don't have to set foot in a church ever again?" Absolutely not! The Bible admonishes us not to forsake the assembling of ourselves together (Hebrews 10:25). The true church is about encouraging one another in the truth. Please get in a church that preaches the entire Bible in light of Jesus Christ. Join a church that puts the focus on Him and not on your shortcomings. I pray that you were saved, healed, and delivered through the reading of this book. Remember, we are not thinking in terms of religiosity anymore, so the term 'salvation' simply means reconciling your spirit to God. Deliverance is reconciling your soul and healing is reconciling your body. Speaking of salvation, if you'd like to accept all the goodness that is made available to you by Christ's sacrifice on the cross, I invite you to pray this short prayer from your heart:

Jesus, thank You so much for all that You have done for me and for giving up Your life so that I could have a life. I believe that You died on the cross for my sins and now I am willing to repent of my sin. I now accept You as my Lord and my Savior, and by faith I receive all of the benefits You died to give me. Thank You, Jesus, for Your unmerited favor and unlimited grace that has saved me from my sins. Transform my life so that I can forever bring glory to Your name and spread Your grace to the world! In Jesus' name, Amen.

If you've prayed that prayer, I believe that Jesus immediately came into your heart. Get ready to get your worldview wrecked for the better!

Now that you've received the message of grace, make sure you do something with it. Grace is not an easy thing to preach. Why? Grace takes all the focus off man and puts it on Jesus. Humans like too much credit. We're all guilty of liking our ego stroked. Human nature is accustomed to getting rewarded for work. For example, if I work 40 hours a week, I should get a certain amount in my paycheck. It's the same way most believe in religion. If I fast for a period of time, God will give me a special revelation that He's never revealed to anyone else. It's almost like we want to say we've earned the right to be close to God. Newsflash, it's not about you, it's about Him! Only a true and living encounter with Jesus Christ is an absolute guarantee to free sinners from their bondage. Belief in Jesus is much more than just trying to escape the dangers of hell. Heaven is not some sort of bribe to get you to believe in Jesus. It's nothing more than an everlasting communion of love with God, the Father. Thus, to be separated from the goodness of God would be absolute hell. Only those who are enemies of God and want nothing to do with Him after a true encounter of grace himself are those who will suffer condemnation. As I begin to end this chapter, I want to admonish you to work out your own salvation before judging someone else's.

May I just encourage you not to quit, give up, or remain in fear? The devil knows God has a plan for your life. He knows God has put purpose, vision, and destiny inside and upon you. He also knows that he can't defeat, destroy, or overcome the power of God's Word in you. Remember, as long as you fight to enter into His rest and hold on to the promises of God, you win. Each time you refuse to allow discouragement and depression to overtake you, you win. Bathe yourself daily in God's Word and prayer. As believers, we are washed by the water of the word. (Ephesians 5:26). Stop walking in the natural and start walking in the supernatural. Living in the spirit should not be a religious colloquialism; it should be a daily reality.

You can escape the religious matrix! You can think for yourself! You can! Why? Because Jesus is Lord and because He is Lord, you CAN do "all things through Christ that strengthens you" (Philippians 4:13). I know it's scary. I know it's hard. I've dealt with the cognitive dissonance, but this freedom, this joy that I feel and will forever experience, was worth every bit of what I went through getting away from the grip that religion had on me. Know that God is for you, and He is with you. When you feel alone or by yourself, He's there. Also know that there are many more just like you who have been down this path, are now on this path, or are about to embrace this new path. Just know that I'm praying for and with you that Jesus will reveal Himself in a way in which you may have never understood Him before. He loves you too much to let you stay in the religious matrix. The good fight of faith is to fight to believe that you have been made righteous by faith and not by effort.

I'm so excited for what's in your future.

Wishing you all the best,

Lesley A. Francisco

Endnotes

CHAPTER 2

1 Chip Brogden, schoolofchrist.org

2 See more at: http://www.patheos.com/blogs/nakedpastor/2013/12/10-reasons-why-abusive-churches-succeed/#sthash.3Dnh4h2c.dpuf

3 Prince, Joseph (2011-05-15). *Destined To Reign* (Kindle Locations 109-114). Kindle Edition.

CHAPTER 3

1 Hay, Louise L. (1984-01-01). *Heal Your Body* (Kindle Locations 102-103). Hay House, Inc. Kindle Edition.

2 Anderson, Neil T. (2006-12-15). *The Bondage Breaker®* (Kindle Locations 4628-4629). Harvest House Publishers. Kindle Edition.

3 Murphy, Joseph (2010-03-20). *The Power of Your Subconscious Mind* (Kindle Locations 502-503). Wilder Publications. Kindle Edition.

CHAPTER 4

1 Even Marais, Cornel (2009-08-01). *So You Think Your Mind Is Renewed?* (Kindle Locations 480-481). New Nature Publications. Kindle Edition.

2 McVey, Steve (2005-05-01). *Grace Walk* (p. 110). Harvest House Publishers. Kindle Edition.

CHAPTER 5

1   Pinnock, Clark H. *A wideness in God's mercy: the finality of Jesus Christ in a world of religions.* Grand Rapids, Mich.: Zondervan, 1992.

2   Marais, Cornel (2009-08-01). *So You Think Your Mind Is Renewed?* (Kindle Locations 204-206). New Nature Publications. Kindle Edition.

3   Jeff-turner.org

4   Strong, James. *Strong's exhaustive concordance of the Bible.* Updated ed. Peabody, MA: Hendrickson Publishers, 2007.

5   Anderson, Neil T. (2006-12-15). *The Bondage Breaker®* (Kindle Locations 646-647). Harvest House Publishers. Kindle Edition.

6   McVey, Steve (2005-05-01). *Grace Walk* (p. 34). Harvest House Publishers. Kindle Edition.

7   *NAS Exhaustive Concordance of the Bible with Hebrew-Aramaic and Greek Dictionaries.* Copyright © 1981, 1998 by The Lockman Foundation.

8   Pinnock, Clark H.. *A wideness in God's mercy: the finality of Jesus Christ in a world of religions.* Grand Rapids, Mich.: Zondervan, 1992, 180.

9   Camps, Arnulf. *Partners in dialogue: Christianity and other world religions.* Maryknoll, NY: Orbis Books, 1983, 139-141.

CHAPTER 6

1   Farley, Andrew (2009-08-25). *The Naked Gospel: Truth You May Never Hear in Church* (p. 101). Zondervan. Kindle Edition.

2   Gill, John. *An exposition of the New Testament in three volumes:* London: Printed for the author, 174648.

3   Joshuatongol.com

4   Anderson, Neil T. (2006-12-15). *The Bondage Breaker®* (Kindle Locations 1097-1099). Harvest House Publishers. Kindle Edition.